Spelling Activity Book 2

How to use this book

The activities in this book are designed to cover the range of skills children need to practise in order to become proficient spellers. Your child will be travelling on an imaginary train, stopping at unusual train stations. Each station focuses on a different spelling pattern. There are things to see and do at each station that help your child practise spelling. Remember the station - remember the spelling!

All aboard! Off we go.

Contents

- ar
- er, er
- ir, ur
- oo (long)
- oo (short)
- oa, oe
- ow /oa/
- ou, ow /ou/
- ue (long /oo/)
- ew /yoo/
- ue /yoo/
- ie /igh/
- oy, oi
- or, ore
- au, aw
- air, ear /ear/
- are /air/
- ear /air/
- ph, wh
- un-
- Compound Words

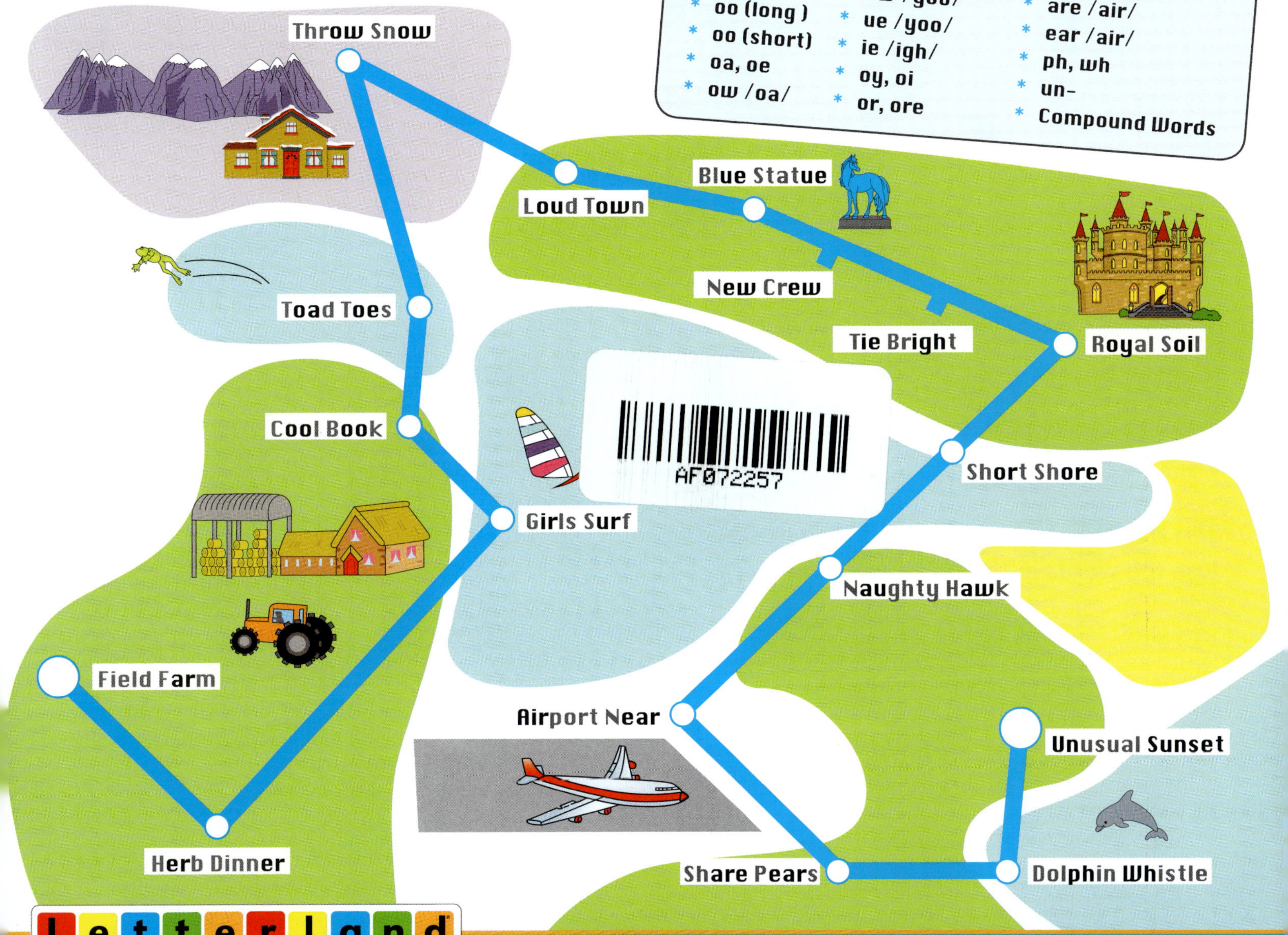

Throw Snow · Loud Town · Blue Statue · Toad Toes · New Crew · Tie Bright · Royal Soil · Cool Book · Girls Surf · Short Shore · Field Farm · Naughty Hawk · Airport Near · Unusual Sunset · Herb Dinner · Share Pears · Dolphin Whistle

[Letterland]

Where you see this symbol, support your child. Read the station name together and talk about the station rule. For the first few pages, work with your child to complete the activities, making sure they know exactly what to do. Use the activities as an opportunity to talk with your child about spelling and vocabulary. You will soon find that they enjoy working through the activities independently.

Support

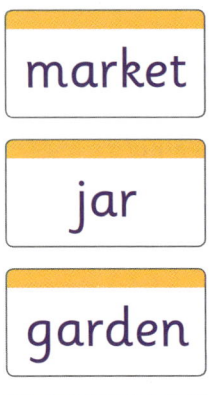

STATION
Field Farm

ar

Match the tickets Draw lines to match the word and picture tickets.

market

jar

garden

car

STATION RULE
The /ar/ sound can be spelt in different ways. For example, ar as in car, al as in calm, and a as in father.

Word train Find and circle four **ar** words in the train.

d c a r h o u s t a r f g a r d e n e m a r k e t

Puzzle Solve the clues to find a mystery word in the red boxes. Use the words in the box to help you.

park   bark   star   March   car

1. See this in the night sky.
2. The month before April.
3. A place to play on the swings.
4. A vehicle with four wheels.
5. The noise a dog makes.

The mystery word is:

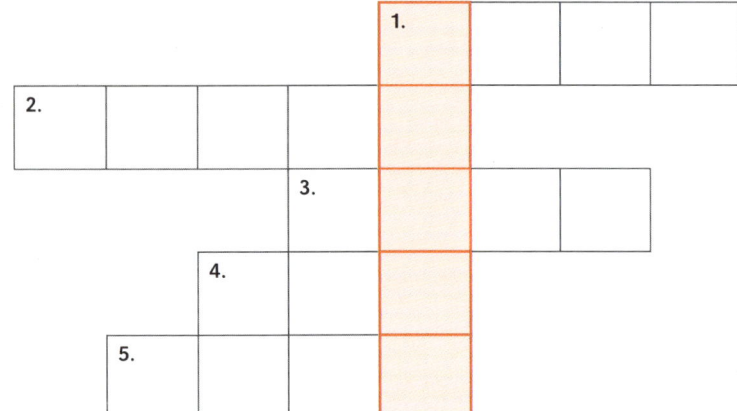

STATION

Herb Dinner

er (stressed and unstressed)

Story Read the story and underline the words that contain **er**.

It was summer and Bertie and his little sister, Jen, were eating dinner on the train. "What shall we do later?" asked Bertie. Jen wanted to dress up and get her mermaid outfit on. Bertie was sad. He had grown taller and his outfits no longer fitted him!

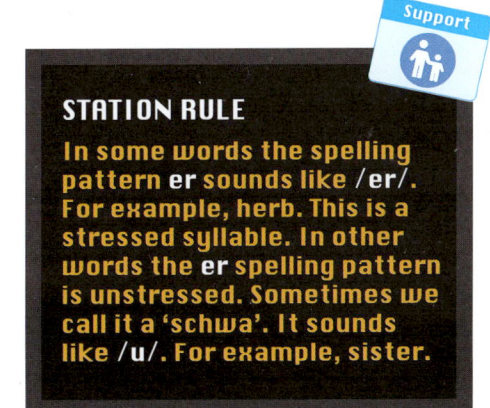

STATION RULE
In some words the spelling pattern er sounds like /er/. For example, herb. This is a stressed syllable. In other words the er spelling pattern is unstressed. Sometimes we call it a 'schwa'. It sounds like /u/. For example, sister.

Window seat Use the words in the word box to write about the view.

| flowers | herbs | under | perfume | mother |

Match the tickets Draw lines to match the word and picture tickets.

bird

skirt

girl

first

STATION RULE
The /er/ sound can be spelt in many different ways. For example, er as in herb, ir as in girl and ur as in turn.

Puzzle Solve the clues to find a mystery word in the red boxes. Use the words in the box to help you.

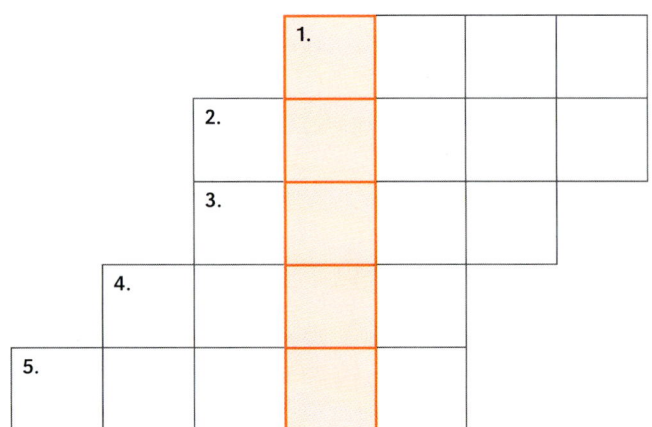

stir   dirty   third   girl   bird

1. Put the ingredients in the bowl and do this.
2. After second.
3. It has two wings and a beak.
4. Not a boy.
5. My boots after a muddy walk.

The mystery word is:

Word train Find and circle four **ir** words in the train.

| s | h | i | r | t | u | t | h | i | r | d | e | a | d | i | r | t | y | s | u | n | s | t | i | r |

4

ur

Story
Read the story and underline the words that contain **ur**.

It was Thursday. Kirsty and her mum met Aunt Silvia at the station. They were going to a burger bar for lunch. Aunt Silvia was a nurse. She looked after people who were hurt.

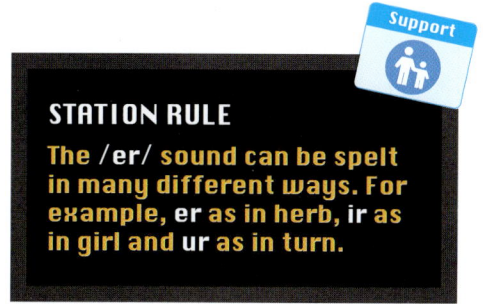

STATION RULE
The /er/ sound can be spelt in many different ways. For example, er as in herb, ir as in girl and ur as in turn.

Window seat
Use the words in the word box to write about the view.

surf   turtle   burn   hurt   purple

STATION
Cool Book

oo, oo

STATION RULE
The spelling pattern **oo** can have a long /oo/ sound as in food, or it can have a short /oo/ sound as in book.

Match the tickets Draw lines to match the word and picture tickets.

goose

hood

boots

crook

Word train Find and circle four **oo** words in the train.

Puzzle Solve the clues to find a mystery word in the red boxes. Use the words in the box to help you.

zoo   cook   moon   room   book

1. Enjoy reading this.
2. A place where your bed is.
3. A place where animals live.
4. Make food hot.
5. See it in the night sky.

The mystery word is:

_____

STATION
Toad Toes

oa, oe

Story Read the story and underline the words that contain **oa** or **oe**.

Joe was having a bad day. First he left his coat on the train. Then on his way to the lost property desk he stubbed his toe. He didn't want to moan, though it hurt. He got his coat back then treated himself to a pudding called an ice-cream float.

STATION RULE
The long vowel sound /oa/ can be spelt in many different ways. For example, oa as in coat, o_e as in rose, ow as in snow and oe as in toe.

Window seat Use the words in the word box to write about the view.

boat doe coach toad goat

STATION
Throw Snow

ow /oa/

Match the tickets Draw lines to match the word and picture tickets.

- elbow
- throw
- grow
- snow

STATION RULE
The long vowel sound /oa/ can be spelt in many different ways. For example, oa as in coat, o_e as in rose, ow as in snow and oe as in toe.

Puzzle Solve the clues to find a mystery word in the red boxes. Use the words in the box to help you.

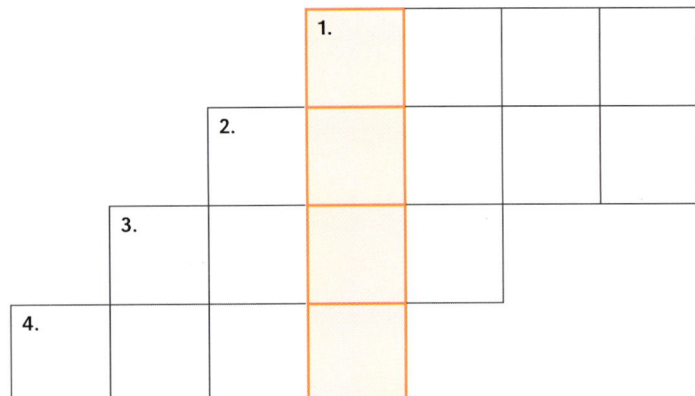

grow   snow   throw   blow

1. Cold and flakey weather.
2. Push a ball through the air.
3. Plants get taller.
4. The wind does this.

The mystery word is:

Word train Find and circle four **ow** words in the train.

a r r o w b l o w g n o s l o w u e t s e l b o w

8

STATION
Loud Town

ou, ow /ou/

Story Read the story and underline the words that contain **ou** or **ow** sounds.

Imran and Zain were getting the train south into town. Imran was feeling down. He had a frown on his forehead and the corners of his mouth were turned down. He soon cheered up when they saw a silly clown on the platform.

STATION RULE
The /ou/ sound can be spelt in different ways. For example, ou as in out and ow as in now.

Window seat Use the words in the word box to write about the view.

mouse   house   frown   shout   gown

STATION
Blue Statue

ue (long /oo/), ue /yoo/

Match the tickets Draw lines to match the word and picture tickets.

- barbecue
- glue
- queue
- clue

STATION RULE
The spelling pattern **ue** can have a long /oo/ sound as in blue, or it can have a /yoo/ sound as in rescue.

Word train Find and circle four **ue** words in the train.

| s | b | l | u | e | n | t | r | u | e | g | u | r | e | s | c | u | e | j | k | a | r | g | u | e |

Puzzle Solve the clues to find a mystery word in the red boxes. Use the words in the box to help you.

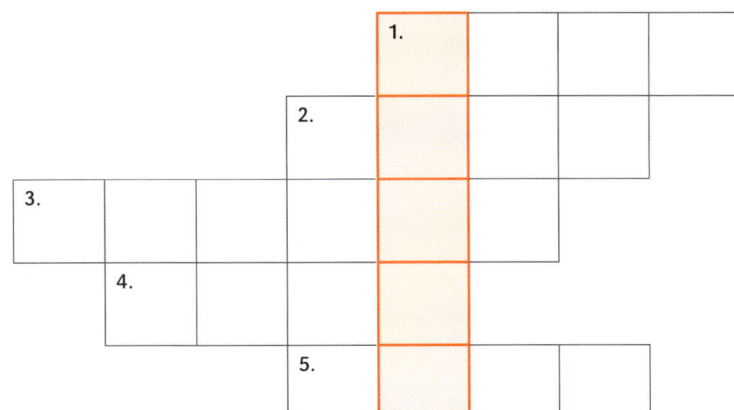

glue   blue   tissue   clue   true

1. This could help you solve a mystery.
2. When the answer is correct.
3. Use this to blow your nose.
4. A cool colour.
5. Use this for sticking things.

The mystery word is:

10

STATION

N ew Crew

ew (long /oo/), ew /yoo/

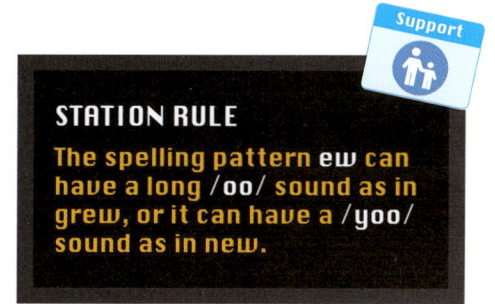

Story Read the story and underline the words that contain **ew**.

Matthew went to visit his newborn nephew. He stopped at the newsagents to get a card and a few pencils. His new nephew was called Andrew McFrew. Matthew drew Andrew.

STATION RULE
The spelling pattern **ew** can have a long /oo/ sound as in grew, or it can have a /yoo/ sound as in new.

Window seat Use the words in the word box to write about the view.

drew   flew   shrew   grew   jewels

11

STATION
Tie Bright

ie

Match the tickets
Draw lines to match the word and picture tickets.

| pie |
| magpie |
| tie |
| tie up |

STATION RULE
The long vowel sound /igh/ can be spelt in many different ways. For example, ie as in tie, igh as in night, i_e as in bike and y as in cry.

Puzzle
Solve the clues to find a mystery word in the red boxes. Use the words in the box to help you.

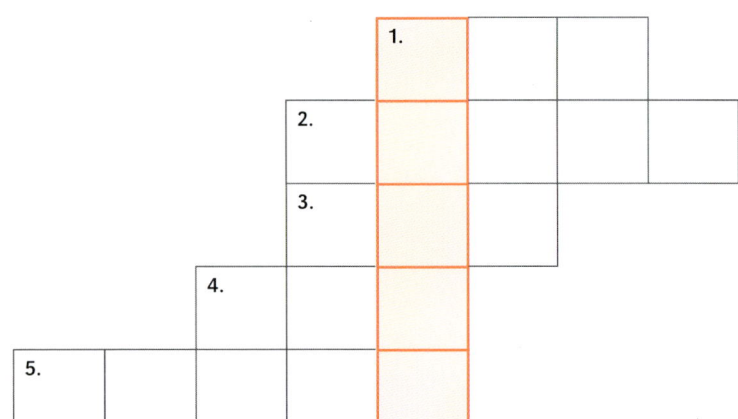

cried   tie   pie   lie   fried

1. Do this to a piece of string to make a knot.
2. How is food cooked in a frying pan?
3. To not tell the truth.
4. Made with pastry and a savoury or sweet filling.
5. What you did sometimes when you were a baby.

The mystery word is:

Word train
Find and circle four **ie** words in the train.

c r i e d a b s t i e g h p i e n o p d r i e d q

igh

Story Read the story and underline the words that contain **igh**.

Sima got a fright. There were toys piled high in her bedroom. It was a terrible sight. As she put everything in the right places a huge spider ran across the floor. She jumped and squeezed her teddy tight.

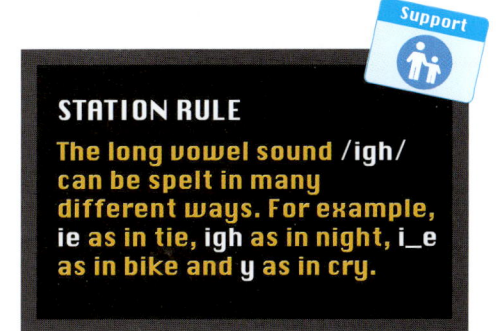

STATION RULE
The long vowel sound /igh/ can be spelt in many different ways. For example, ie as in tie, igh as in night, i_e as in bike and y as in cry.

Window seat Use the words in the word box to write about the view.

knight night flight bright light

_____

_____

_____

_____

STATION Royal Soil

oi

Match the tickets
Draw lines to match the word and picture tickets.

toilet

point

oil

coin

STATION RULE
The spelling pattern **oi** is virtually never used at the end of words.

Word train
Find and circle four **oi** words in the train.

p o i n t a t o i l e t b c a v o i d e b o i l f

Puzzle
Solve the clues to find a mystery word in the red boxes. Use the words in the box to help you.

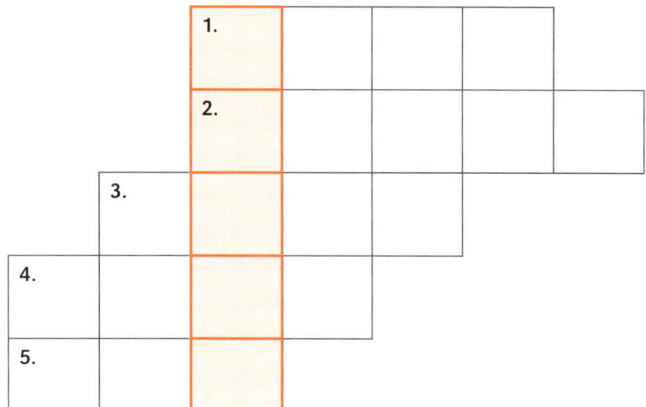

| point oil soil boil coin |

1. Find this in the garden.
2. Use your finger to show the way.
3. Make the water very hot indeed.
4. A small valuable round disc.
5. Use this for cooking.

The mystery word is:

14

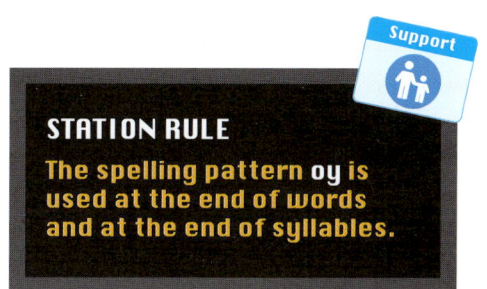

Story Read the story and underline the words that contain **oy**.

The royal family employed Toyah to help them on voyages. Toyah loved to eat oysters. Her loyal dog, Rufus, preferred to eat soya. Rufus was usually good but today he had destroyed a magazine and scattered its pages all over the train.

STATION RULE
The spelling pattern **oy** is used at the end of words and at the end of syllables.

Window seat Use the words in the word box to write about the view.

Roy   toy   boy   annoyed   enjoyed

STATION
Short Shore

or

Match the tickets
Draw lines to match the word and picture tickets.

- horse
- corn
- fork
- story

STATION RULE
The sound /or/ can be spelt in many different ways. The most common spelling patterns for the /or/ sound are **or** as in **fork** and **ore** as in **more**.

Puzzle
Solve the clues to find a mystery word in the red boxes. Use the words in the box to help you.

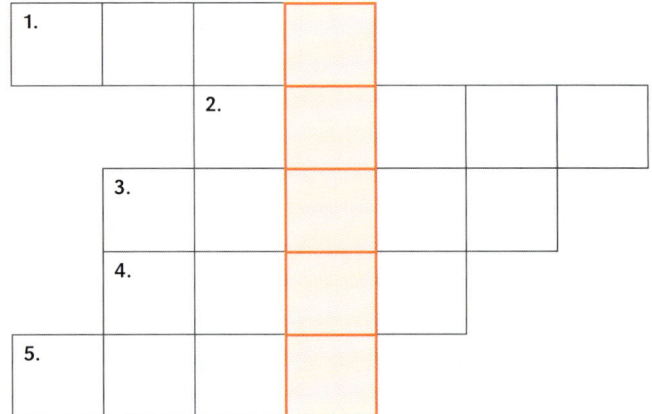

sort   storm   corn   short   fork

1. This means the same as 'tidy up'.
2. Not tall.
3. Thunder, lightening, wind and rain.
4. Eat your dinner using this.
5. A yellow vegetable.

The mystery word is:
_____

Word train
Find and circle four **or** words in the train.

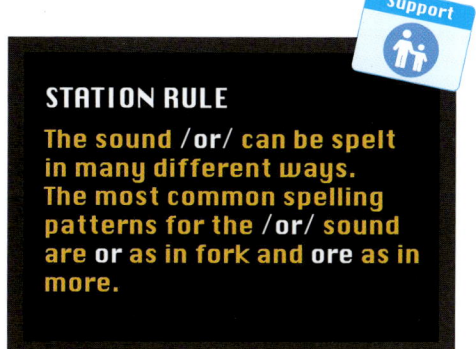

Story Read the story and underline the words that contain **ore**.

Before sunset, Scott was on his way home from the superstore. He wore the new boots he bought. He looked out of the window at the seashore and thought about how much he adored living here.

STATION RULE
The sound /or/ can be spelt in many different ways. The most common spelling patterns for the /or/ sound are **or** as in fork and **ore** as in more.

Window seat Use the words in the word box to write about the view.

chore   core   store   snore   more

STATION
Naughty Hawk

au

Match the tickets
Draw lines to match the word and picture tickets.

- dinosaur
- astronaut
- sauce
- launch

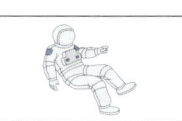

STATION RULE
The spelling pattern **au** is used at the beginning or in the middle or words for the /au/ sound.

Word train
Find and circle four **au** words in the train.

a u t h o r n a u g h t y d i n o s a u r h a u l

Puzzle
Solve the clues to find a mystery word in the red boxes. Use the words in the box to help you.

astronaut haul
taut dinosaur
autumn sauce

1. The season before winter.
2. A tasty liquid.
3. To pull something tight.
4. A pile of stolen treasure.
5. This person goes to space.
6. A pre-historic creature.

The mystery word is: _____

aw

Story
Read the story and underline the words that contain **aw**.

Dawn kept busy on her train ride by drawing lots of pictures. She had drawn a fawn with its mummy lying next to a bush. She nibbled on raw carrot sticks. Later in the car, Dawn looked out of the window and saw a real herd of deer.

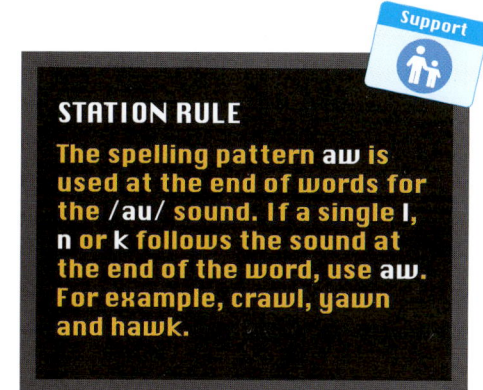

STATION RULE
The spelling pattern aw is used at the end of words for the /au/ sound. If a single l, n or k follows the sound at the end of the word, use aw. For example, crawl, yawn and hawk.

Window seat
Use the words in the word box to write about the view.

yawn   shawl   awful   paw   thaw

_____
_____
_____
_____

STATION
Airport N**ear**

air, ear

Match the tickets Draw lines to match the word and picture tickets.

aircraft

tear

hair

hear

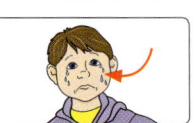
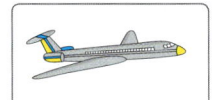

STATION RULE

The sound /air/ can be spelt in different ways. For example, air as in hair, are as in care and ear as in bear. The letters ear can represent the sound /ear/ as in dear but they can also represent the sounds /air/ as in bear and /er/ as in earth.

Puzzle Solve the clues to find a mystery word in the red boxes. Use the words in the box to help you.

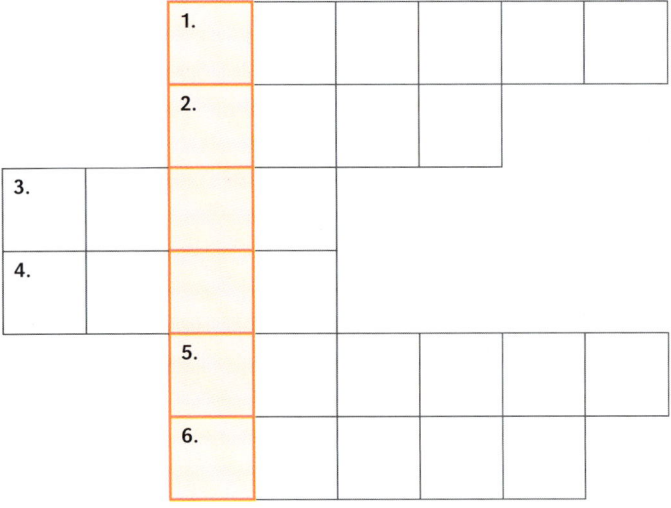

tear   spear   pair   repair   shears   year

1. Scissors for cutting sheep's wool.
2. This comes from your eye when you cry.
3. 365 days.
4. Two items that go together, like socks.
5. To fix something.
6. A long stick with a pointed tip.

The mystery word is: _____

Word train Find and circle four **air** or **ear** words in the train.

20

STATION: Share Pears

are, ear

Story Read the story and underline the words that contain **are** or **ear**.

Daddy paid the train fare and the family boarded the train. People stared at his jumper because it had a great big tear down one sleeve. Daddy didn't care. The family had been on a tree climbing activity day and he had nothing else to wear.

STATION RULE
The sound /air/ can be spelt in different ways. For example, air as in hair, are as in care and ear as in bear.

Window seat Use the words in the word box to write about the view.

bear   pear   hare   mare   share

STATION
Dolphin Whistle

ph

Match the tickets Draw lines to match the word and picture tickets.

dolphin

elephant

alphabet

trophy

a b c d e f g h i j
k l m n o p q r s
t u v w x y z

Support

STATION RULE
The usual way to spell the /f/ sound is with **f**, but some less common words need **ph** instead.

Word train Find and circle four **ph** words in the train.

d o l p h i n d p h o n e u p h o t o t r o p h y

Puzzle Solve the clues to find a mystery word in the red boxes. Use the words in the box to help you.

photo   elephant
alphabet
dolphin   trophy

1. Say cheese to have your picture taken.
2. 26 letter shapes.
3. An award for success.
4. A friendly sea animal.
5. A large grey four-legged animal.

The mystery word is:

22

wh

Story Read the story and underline the words that contain **wh**.

Miss White reminded the children to whisper as they chose where to sit on the train. "What a wonderful visit to the museum that was," she said. The children whispered to each other about which exhibit was the best and why they liked it.

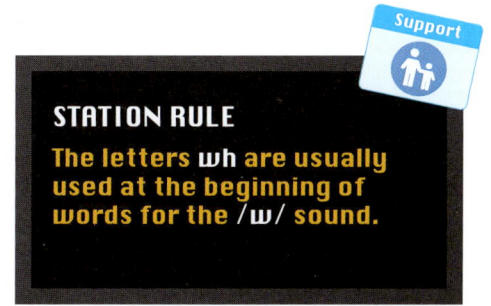

STATION RULE
The letters **wh** are usually used at the beginning of words for the /w/ sound.

Window seat Use the words in the word box to write about the view.

whale   when   where   what   whistle

STATION
Unusual Sunset

un-, Compound Words

Match the tickets Draw lines to match the compound word tickets. Then write the compound words in the box at the side.

STATION RULE
The prefix **un-** is added to the beginning of a word without any change to the spelling of the root word.

Compound words are two words joined together. Each part of the longer word is spelt as it would be if it were on its own.

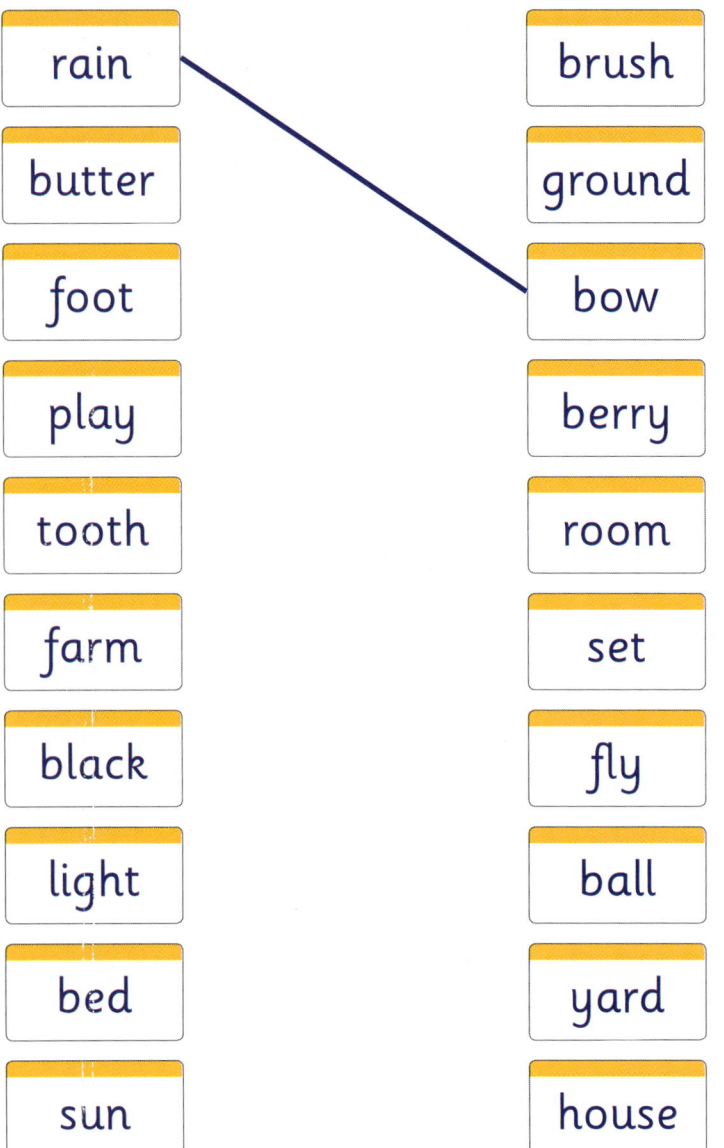

rainbow

Word train Find and circle four **un-** words in the train.

| u | n | h | a | p | p | y | u | n | l | o | a | d | u | n | l | o | c | k | u | n | w | e | l | l |

24